TRANSCENDING RACE IN AMERICA
BIOGRAPHIES OF BIRACIAL ACHIEVERS

Halle Berry

Beyoncé

David Blaine

Mariah Carey

Frederick Douglass

W. E. B. Du Bois

Salma Hayek

Derek Jeter

Alicia Keys

Soledad O'Brien

Rosa Parks

Prince

Booker T. Washington

W.E.B. Du BOIS

Civil Rights Activist, Author, Historian

Jim Whiting

Mason Crest Publishers

Produced by 21st Century Publishing and Communications, Inc.

MASON CREST PUBLISHERS INC.
370 Reed Road
Broomall, Pennsylvania 19008
(866) MCP-BOOK (toll free)
www.masoncrest.com

Printed in the United States of America.

First Printing

9 8 7 6 5 4 3 2 1

Library of Congress Cataloging-in-Publication Data

Whiting, Jim, 1943–
    W.E.B. Du Bois : civil rights activist, author, historian / Jim Whiting.
       p. cm.
    Includes bibliographical references and index.
    ISBN 978-1-4222-1618-7 (hardback : alk. paper) — ISBN 978-1-4222-1632-3 (pbk. : alk. paper)
    1. Du Bois, W. E. B. (William Edward Burghardt), 1868–1963—Juvenile literature. 2. African
Americans—Biography—Juvenile literature. 3. African American intellectuals—Biography—
Juvenile literature. 4. African American civil rights workers—Biography—Juvenile literature.
I. Title.
E185.97.D73W55 2010
303.48'4092—dc22
[B]   2009022049

Table of Contents

"I HAVE BROTHERS, SISTERS, NIECES, NEPHEWS, UNCLES, AND COUSINS, OF EVERY RACE AND EVERY HUE, SCATTERED ACROSS THREE CONTINENTS, AND FOR AS LONG AS I LIVE, I WILL NEVER FORGET THAT IN NO OTHER COUNTRY ON EARTH IS MY STORY EVEN POSSIBLE."

"WE MAY HAVE DIFFERENT STORIES, BUT WE HOLD COMMON HOPES. . . . WE MAY NOT LOOK THE SAME AND WE MAY NOT HAVE COME FROM THE SAME PLACE, BUT WE ALL WANT TO MOVE IN THE SAME DIRECTION — TOWARDS A BETTER FUTURE . . ."

— BARACK OBAMA, 44TH PRESIDENT
OF THE UNITED STATES OF AMERICA

Chapter

1

❦

90
AND STILL
GOING STRONG

MORE THAN 1,000 GUESTS JAMMED THE
ballroom of the Roosevelt Hotel in New York City on
the evening of March 2, 1958. All of them wanted to
pay tribute to William Edward Burghardt (usually
abbreviated W.E.B.) Du Bois (pronounced due
BOYSS) on his 90th birthday. "It was an excited and
happy gathering," wrote W.E.B.'s wife Shirley.

The tributes weren't limited to the people in the ballroom.
They poured in from all around the world: China, the Soviet
Union, India, Great Britain, France, Brazil, and many other
countries. Nnandi Azikiwe, **premier** of Eastern Nigeria,
expressed the feelings of many people when he wrote,

> "Your life has been an inspiration to us who are now
> in the **vanguard** of the great struggle for freedom
> in Africa."

W.E.B. Du Bois, still an active speaker and author, celebrates his 90th birthday with his wife and friends in 1958. W.E.B. was an early leader in the cause of racial equality. Over his long life, he worked tirelessly to make sure black people could achieve their goals—socially, economically, and politically.

Some of the tributes took a very practical form. W.E.B. wasn't a wealthy man, and he needed money to work on several of his projects. The guests donated a total of more than $7,500 to him. That's over $55,000 in today's dollars.

A LIFE FULL OF ACCOMPLISHMENTS

There was plenty to honor. W.E.B. was the first African American to earn a Ph.D. degree from Harvard University. As a university professor, he influenced the lives of countless numbers of students. He was also a noted author who wrote more than 20 books.

W.E.B. works in his office at the Council on African Affairs in New York City, 1954. Not only was he the first African American to get a Ph.D. from Harvard, but he also became a professor, an author, and a co-founder of the NAACP. Everything he did advanced the principle of racial justice.

W.E.B. was especially famous as one of the earliest figures in the struggle for racial equality. More than a half a century before the U.S. Supreme Court ruled that the nation's schools could no longer be segregated, more than half a century before Rosa Parks began the Birmingham bus boycott that catapulted Dr. Martin Luther King Jr. to national prominence, W.E.B. was working tirelessly on behalf of black people.

He co-founded the National Association for the Advancement of Colored People (NAACP). He edited the organization's monthly magazine, *The Crisis*. He continually spoke out for racial justice.

Above all, W.E.B. always remained true to his personal beliefs. In recent years, some of these beliefs had become unpopular. Biographer David Levering Lewis says W.E.B "conceded mischievously that he would have been hailed with approval if he had died at fifty. 'At seventy-five my death was practically requested.'"

WORDS TO LIVE BY

W.E.B. Du Bois was still very much alive. After several dignitaries gave speeches praising him, he approached the podium to thunderous applause. Perhaps the oldest person in the room, he directed his remarks to the youngest—his two-year-old great-grandson, Arthur McFarlane II:

> **"The return from your work must be the satisfaction which that work brings you and the world's need of that work. Income is not greenbacks, it is satisfaction; it is creation; it is beauty. It is the supreme sense of a world of men going forward, lurch and stagger though it may, but slowly, inevitably going forward, and you, yourself with your hands on the wheel. Make this choice then, my son. Never hesitate, never falter."**

A TALE OF MANY CITIES

The evening at the Roosevelt was just the beginning. For the next six weeks, W.E.B. and his wife traveled across the country for additional gatherings. One of the largest was in Chicago, where the guests presented him with another check. And these events weren't all fancy banquets where everyone dressed up. As his wife noted,

> **"Besides the big public affairs in every city, there were numerous home parties, sometimes with lavish spreads, sometimes with young, enthusiastic, struggling art or literary groups. Du Bois refused no invitations—and he enjoyed every gathering."**

As part of his 90th birthday celebration in 1958, W.E.B. was honored at graduation ceremonies at Fisk University, where he had graduated in 1888. Current students welcomed him into the school's chapter of the national honor society, Phi Beta Kappa.

The honors **culminated** in May. He had graduated from Fisk University in Nashville, Tennessee, in 1888. The school's current president, S.J. Wright, invited W.E.B. to come to the school for its **commencement** ceremony. According to Wright,

> "During the past sixty-five years, few men have done as much as you have to lift the social, economic and civil horizons of the Negro, and the recognition being accorded to you at this time is, in some measure, an expression of gratitude to a great man from an appreciative racial group."

He said Fisk would present W.E.B. with a citation and ask for a response, but there would be no other demands on him. That turned out to be not quite true.

STILL ANOTHER HONOR

A group of Fisk students inducted W.E.B. into the school's chapter of Phi Beta Kappa, the national honor society for the very best college and university students. For Shirley, it was about time. She wrote,

> "When he went on to graduate from Harvard University and take two graduate degrees there, it was unthinkable to accept a Negro student into this oldest of American college fraternities, regardless of his scholastic record. The Fisk chapter decided to correct this omission."

"Correcting the omission" went both ways. A few weeks later, the Fisk librarian wrote to W.E.B., "We were greatly stimulated by your presence here, and we look forward eagerly to other sessions."

Most people at W.E.B.'s age would have been content to settle down after hearing so many nice things being said about them. But W.E.B. Du Bois had never been "most people." He was about to begin an entirely new chapter of his life.

Chapter

2

❖

GETTING
A GOOD
EDUCATION

W.E.B. DU BOIS DESCRIBED HIS BACKGROUND as "a flood of Negro blood, a strain of French, a bit of Dutch, but, thank God! No 'Anglo-Saxon.'" Much of the "Negro blood" came from his mother, Mary Burghardt. She was descended from a slave who served in the Revolutionary War and became free. Her family owned a farm in Great Barrington, Massachusetts.

A trickle of Negro blood and all the rest came from his father, Alfred Du Bois. Alfred's grandfather James was a white man who owned a plantation in the Bahamas Islands. James had several sons with one of his slaves. One of those sons named Alexander, in turn, fathered Alfred.

It's not clear how Alfred came to Great Barrington and met Mary. They were married in 1867 and W.E.B. was born on

W.E.B. (bottom right) felt lucky to grow up without racism among free blacks in Massachusetts. His grandfather Alexander (top left) and his father Alfred (top right) had a mixture of French, Dutch, and black ancestors; his mother Mary Sylvina (holding baby W.E.B.) was descended from a slave.

February 23, 1868. The Burghardts didn't like Alfred. That might have been one reason why Alfred left his little family behind before W.E.B. was two. "They practically drove him away," he recalled.

It may have been for the better. His mother's emphasis on hard work and getting a good education didn't have any competition.

AN OUTSTANDING STUDENT

From the beginning W.E.B. did well in school. And it wasn't just in the classroom. As he told his wife many years later,

> **"Only now do I realize how fortunate I was in having been born in that particular place, where my family had been for so many generations. I know that I enjoyed a free and happy childhood. All the woods, the hills, and the river belonged to me and the companions of my own age."**

There was very little obvious racism in Great Barrington. For nearly a century, blacks had been free people.

Blacks: Free in the North, Slaves in the South

Blacks originally came to the United States as slaves, both in the North and South. In 1780, Massachusetts became the first state to abolish slavery. Other northern states soon followed.

Conditions were different in the South. Its economy depended on large plantations that grew crops such as cotton, sugar, and tobacco. White plantation owners said they needed slave labor to grow those crops.

The northern states grew increasingly angry because of slavery in the South. The differences between the two sides finally led to the Civil War and the freeing of the slaves in the South.

Even after Civil War, many blacks in the South remained virtual slaves. They were uneducated and had almost no money. As a result, they had to work as **sharecroppers** for their former masters.

Yet W.E.B. couldn't escape racism completely. He had evidence of its existence when he was 10 years old:

"Something put it into the boys' and girls' heads to buy gorgeous visiting-cards—ten cents a package—and exchange. The exchange was merry, until one girl, a tall newcomer, refused my card. . . . Then it dawned upon me with a certain suddenness that I was different from the others."

Southern plantation owners depended on slaves like those pictured here to work in the fields. Northern states had abolished slavery and tried to get the South to do the same. Differences in the economies of the two regions, along with the issue of slavery, eventually led to the Civil War.

PEOPLE ARE ALL ALIKE

This slight may have spurred W.E.B. He later wrote,

> **"I very early got the idea that what I was going to do was to prove to the world that Negroes were just like other people."**

In high school, W.E.B. went beyond "other people." Besides getting top grades, he worked at several jobs. He also wrote articles for two newspapers and edited the school newspaper.

His attitude and work ethic impressed several townspeople, in particular Principal Frank Hosmer. Hardly anyone in Great

W.E.B. (far left) poses with his high school classmates, around 1884. Although he did very well in school, he couldn't go to Harvard, which was close by. He didn't have enough money but, more importantly, Harvard didn't admit black students.

Barrington went to college from high school. In addition, W.E.B. didn't have any money. Yet Hosmer encouraged him to take college prep courses. The wife of a mill owner provided crucial assistance by buying the expensive books he needed for his courses. He recalled,

> **"I accepted the offer as something normal and right; only after many years did I realize how critical this gift was for my career."**

W.E.B. wanted to go to Harvard, not far away in Massachusetts. Lack of money wasn't the only problem. His mother had had a stroke while he was still young and her health was steadily declining. So even though he graduated in 1884 at the age of 16, he stayed home and took care of her. She died in March 1885. While W.E.B. was heartbroken, her death allowed him to leave Great Barrington.

GOING TO COLLEGE

W.E.B. wouldn't go to Harvard because it was very expensive. And like most colleges in that era, it was reluctant to admit a black man.

So Hosmer convinced four churches to pledge enough money to let W.E.B. attend Fisk University, a school founded by Congregational ministers in Nashville, Tennessee.

It was 1885, and W.E.B. Du Bois was about to enter the "real world."

Despite his disappointment at not going to Harvard, W.E.B. looked forward to an adventure. He later wrote,

> **"I was going into the South; the South of slavery, rebellion and black folk; above all, I was going to meet colored people of my own age and education, of my own ambitions."**

GETTING A HEAD START

Right away he got a break. Fisk liked the quality of his high school education and enrolled him as a sophomore. He became very popular among his fellow students and continued his interest in journalism by editing the school newspaper. He often used it to state his views.

Fisk University

The Fisk School was founded in January 1866, by white missionaries in small **ramshackle** wooden structures. About a year and a half later it was incorporated as Fisk University. Upwards of 1,000 blacks—ranging in age from 7 to 70 and eager for the chance to learn—began attending.

The institution fell deeply in debt. In 1871, the Fisk Jubilee Choir took all the school's money and began a tour in the United States and Europe. The choir raised enough money to pay off the debt, buy new property, and build Jubilee Hall, a solid brick building. To this day, the university honors October 6, the anniversary of their departure.

When W.E.B. arrived, it was the country's best-known black university. Admissions standards had risen, and the number of students dropped to about 450. There were 15 instructors.

In 1952, Fisk became the first predomi-nately black university to be granted a chapter of Phi Beta Kappa, the national honor society.

Today, Fisk occupies nearly 30 buildings on a 40-acre campus. Eighty faculty members work with more than 800 students.

He taught at a black school in the countryside outside Nashville during summer vacation. Conditions were primitive. His teacher's desk was three boards. He borrowed his chair and had to return it every night. His students had almost no books. W.E.B. wrote,

> **"I saw the hard, ugly drudgery of country life and the writhing of landless, ignorant peasants. I saw the race problem at nearly its lowest terms."**

DECIDING TO HELP OTHER BLACKS

His teaching experiences convinced him that his destiny lay in helping his fellow blacks. When he spoke at his graduation from Fisk in 1888, he chose German **chancellor** Otto von Bismarck as his subject. Known as the "Iron Chancellor," Bismarck had managed to unite many small kingdoms and forge the modern nation of Germany by sheer force of will and clever politics. W.E.B. didn't agree with all of Bismarck's methods, but he admired the final result:

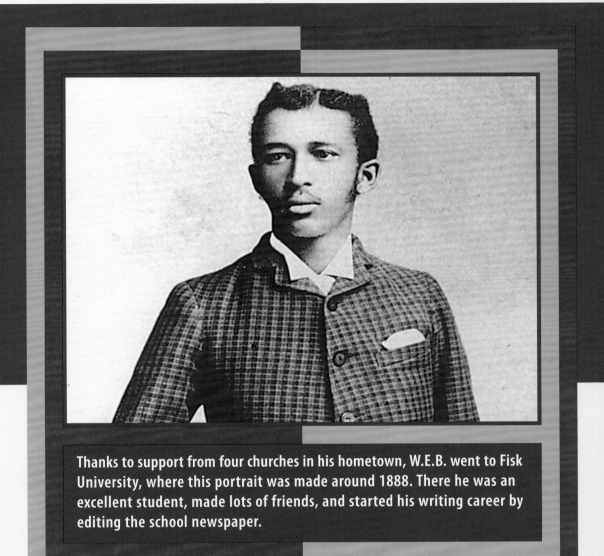

Thanks to support from four churches in his hometown, W.E.B. went to Fisk University, where this portrait was made around 1888. There he was an excellent student, made lots of friends, and started his writing career by editing the school newspaper.

"Bismarck was my hero. He had made a nation out of a mass of bickering peoples. . . . This foreshadowed in my mind the kind of thing American Negroes must do, marching forth with strength and determination under trained leadership."

W.E.B. recognized that his Fisk education was somewhat limited. He knew he needed more. He wrote,

"I wanted the largest and best in organized learning. Nothing could be too big and thorough for training the leadership of the American Negro."

GETTING INTO HARVARD

In his eyes, that meant Harvard. His timing was good. The school had recently decided to make its student body geographically and racially diverse. W.E.B. had to enroll as a junior because Harvard didn't think much of his Fisk degree.

W.E.B. (2nd row from top, 3rd from left) poses with the Harvard class of 1890. After he became Harvard's first black graduate, he stayed on to get a master's degree, started a Ph.D., and then studied in Germany, where he was amazed by the lack of racism he encountered.

He did very well academically, impressing his professors with his intellect. But he deliberately stayed apart from white students because he didn't want to become a part of the white world.

He graduated in 1890 and was one of six students selected to speak at commencement. His speech was well received and led to other speaking invitations.

W.E.B. wasn't ready to leave Harvard. He received a fellowship that allowed him to stay there for two more years. He earned a master's degree and began working on a Ph.D. When the two years were up, he received a grant to study overseas. W.E.B. chose the University of Berlin in Germany, partly because of his admiration for Bismarck.

GOING OVERSEAS

Living and studying in Europe was a revelation. There was very little obvious racism, and W.E.B. found that people judged him on his intellect rather than the color of his skin. He returned the favor: "Slowly they became, not white folks, but folks."

All his life experiences came together on February 23, 1893, when he turned 25. That evening he wrote in his diary,

> **"These are my plans . . . to make a name in science, to make a name in literature and thus to raise my race. Or perhaps to raise a visible empire in Africa thro' England, France, or Germany."**

Though he wanted to stay longer in Berlin, his grant expired in 1894 and he came home. W.E.B. was anxious to put the goals he had written in his diary into practice. Teaching seemed the best way to begin. He received an offer from Wilberforce University in Ohio to teach Latin and Greek.

In what little spare time he had, W.E.B. completed work on his Ph.D. and it was granted the following year. He became the first African American to obtain a Ph.D. degree from Harvard. He was about to embark on a long career that would make him world famous.

Chapter

3

❦

ESTABLISHING HIS REPUTATION

W.E.B. SOON REALIZED THAT WILBERFORCE wasn't a good fit. The school was very conservative, and professors didn't encourage independent thinking. Classes were often interrupted or canceled so students could attend church services. W.E.B. did the best he could. The school had one attraction: a student named Nina Gomer. The couple was married in July 1896.

That wasn't the only good thing in his life that year. Harvard published his **doctoral dissertation**. The book received excellent reviews and began to establish his reputation as an outstanding researcher.

Better news soon followed. The University of Pennsylvania offered him a job for a year. The school is in Philadelphia, and W.E.B.'s responsibility was to study a black neighborhood. It was a slum with a high crime rate and extreme poverty. Philadelphia civic leaders wanted to see the factors that made it such a terrible place.

W.E.B., shown here in a formal portrait, saw his academic reputation grow at the turn of the 20th century. His research at Harvard and the University of Pennsylvania was well received, he was hired by the University of Atlanta, and he became known as an important speaker at home and in Europe.

W.E.B. went through the neighborhood block by block, interviewing more than 5,000 people. He wanted to gather enough information so "we might *know* instead of *think* about the Negro problems."

KNOWING, NOT THINKING

At that time, many whites *thought* blacks were biologically inferior. Many *thought* blacks were almost identical to each other.

W.E.B.'s research exploded these and other assumptions—including his own. "I had learned far more from Philadelphia

This photo, titled "Negro Quarters," appeared on the cover of W.E.B.'s book *The Philadelphia Negro* and shows the heart of black Philadelphia in the 1890s. At the time, Philadelphia had the largest African-American population in the North and was the focus of W.E.B.'s groundbreaking research study.

Negroes than I had taught them concerning the Negro Problem," he wrote.

Much more importantly, he concluded,

> **The centre and kernel of the Negro problem is the narrow opportunities afforded Negroes for earning a decent living. . . . No matter how well-trained a Negro may be, or how fitted for work of any kind, he cannot in the ordinary course of competition hope to be much more than a menial servant.**

He soon had first-hand experience of this conclusion. In spite of his painstaking work, the University of Pennsylvania refused to consider him for further work when his year's appointment was over.

MOVING TO ATLANTA

Pennsylvania's loss was the University of Atlanta's gain. Impressed by his research skills, the school hired him as professor of history and economics. In addition, he would lead a series of yearly conferences focusing on issues facing urban blacks.

He moved to Atlanta in the fall of 1897, accompanied by Nina and Burghardt Gomer Du Bois, the couple's first child. The little boy had been born on October 2.

Historically Black Colleges and Universities

Atlanta University, Fisk, and Wilberforce are all historically black colleges and universities (HBCU). According to the Higher Education Act of 1965, an HBCU is "any historically Black college or university that was established prior to 1964, whose principal mission was, and is, the education of Black Americans."

Currently there are more than a hundred HBCUs. Many were founded in the years following the Civil War. At that time most other colleges were either closed entirely to blacks or only admitted a few. HBCUs allowed blacks to obtain a good education.

While many blacks today attend integrated colleges and universities, others choose to attend an HBCU. Civil rights leader Dr. Martin Luther King Jr., Supreme Court Justice Thurgood Marshall, and Nobel Prize-winning diplomat Ralph Bunch are just a few of the many distinguished blacks who have graduated from HBCUs.

W.E.B, his wife Nina Gomer, and their son Burghardt Gomer lived in Atlanta in 1897. His work on racial discrimination was sadly intertwined with his personal life when a white doctor refused to treat Burghardt and the little boy died of diphtheria.

The job was one of the major turning points of W.E.B.'s life. As he wrote,

> **"My real life work was begun at Atlanta for 13 years, from my 29th to my 42nd birthday. They were years of great spiritual upturning, of the making and unmaking of ideals, of hard work and hard play. Here I found myself."**

A major part of finding himself involved the realization that "the cure [to problems blacks faced] wasn't simply telling people the truth, it was inducing them to act on the truth."

In the South at that time, acting on the truth could be dangerous. In 1896, the Supreme Court handed down its *Plessy* v. *Ferguson* decision. As a result, the number of **Jim Crow laws** was increasing. Even worse, white mobs often took the law into their own hands.

Plessy v. Ferguson

Starting in the late 1870s, southern states began passing Jim Crow laws. Many of these laws said blacks couldn't use the same public facilities as whites. These laws set up the idea of "separate but equal." In reality, facilities for blacks were rarely equal to those for whites.

In 1890, Louisiana passed the Separate Car Act. Under its terms, blacks couldn't travel in the same railroad cars as whites. Homer Plessy, a black man, deliberately broke the law in 1892 so it could be challenged at the U.S. Supreme Court.

By a 7-1 vote in 1896, the U.S. Supreme Court upheld the Separate Car Act. As a result, many more separate but equal laws were passed.

In 1954, the unanimous Supreme Court decision in *Brown* v. *Board of Education of Topeka* said, "separate educational facilities are inherently unequal." It basically overturned *Plessy* v. *Ferguson*.

A HORRIBLE LYNCHING

In April, 1899, W.E.B. was jolted by the lynching of a black man named Sam Hose. Hose killed a white man during an argument. A mob of 2,000 whites burned Hose alive and cut his charred body into little pieces to serve as souvenirs. Some people even sold the pieces to friends who hadn't been "lucky" enough to see the horror firsthand.

W.E.B. walked toward the offices of the local newspaper to hand-deliver a sober, objective editorial he wrote about the evils of lynching. On the way, he passed Hose's blackened knuckles on display in a store window. He turned around and came home. He realized that

❝one could not be a calm, cool, and detached scientist while Negroes were lynched, murdered, and starved.❞

The following month, W.E.B.'s son Burghardt became ill with diphtheria. He died after several white doctors refused to treat him. Whites shouted racial slurs at the parents as they carried the tiny coffin. The tragedy put a strain on their marriage. Some of W.E.B.'s biographers believe his wife never forgave him.

To help overcome his sorrow, W.E.B. threw himself into his work. Later that year his Philadelphia study was published. Called *The Philadelphia Negro*, the book was nearly 1,000 pages long. Many scholarly journals gave it favorable reviews.

A GROWING REPUTATION

With his reputation continuing to grow, W.E.B. received numerous speaking invitations. In 1900, he was invited to the Paris Exposition to set up an exhibit. The exhibit highlighted black achievements and won a gold medal.

The following month W.E.B. attended a Pan-African conference in London, England. The theme of the conference was uniting people of African descent throughout the world. W.E.B. gave a major address.

In October, his wife gave birth to Yolande, their second child. Her arrival helped overcome the sadness that W.E.B. and Nina felt over Burghardt's death.

By then W.E.B. had emerged as an important voice in black affairs. Soon he would come into conflict with the most powerful black man in America at the time: Booker T. Washington.

Washington came to prominence in 1895 when he gave a speech in Atlanta. He urged blacks to put their efforts into learning useful trades. Equal rights with whites could wait. That was welcome news to the country's white leaders. They began consulting him when they needed to make decisions involving living and working conditions for blacks.

RIGHTS NOW, NOT LATER

W.E.B. disagreed with Washington. He thought blacks needed equal rights, and they needed them right away. He was particularly upset that Washington seemed to adopt the attitude of "my way or the highway." Washington used his power to put down blacks who disagreed with him.

The conflict escalated in 1903 when W.E.B. published one of his most famous books, *The Souls of Black Folk.* W.E.B. advocated the "talented tenth." The top ten percent of blacks should be encouraged to go to college to develop the knowledge and skills they would need to assume leadership roles after they graduated.

Another part of the book attacked Washington directly. It made the point that Washington had become the primary black leader because whites approved of him so much. W.E.B. accused him of practically accepting "the **alleged** inferiority of the Negro races."

W.E.B. (right) poses with other faculty members at the University of Atlanta in the 1900s. During his 13 years as a professor there, W.E.B. felt he had found himself. He also realized that his goal would always be to spur people to fight against racism.

Booker T. Washington

Booker T. Washington was born in 1856 in Virginia. His father was a white slave owner, and his mother was a slave. Freed after the Civil War, he moved to West Virginia with his mother and siblings. Because he was a hard worker, his white employer encouraged him to go to school.

Washington used his education to become a teacher. In 1881 he became the first black man to serve as a school principal. Under his direction, Tuskegee Institute became one of the leading black colleges.

He believed strongly that blacks needed education and work skills to advance. He thought gaining those skills was more important than equality with whites.

His 1901 autobiography *Up From Slavery* became one of the most famous books ever written by a black man. That same year Washington became the first African American to be invited to the White House.

Washington's hectic travel schedule and tireless efforts on behalf of black education were very draining. He died in 1915 at the age of 59.

COMING TO A BOIL

Things came to a head in 1905 when Washington gave a speech in Boston. Monroe Trotter, one of W.E.B.'s friends, asked some tough questions. There was pushing and shoving and Trotter was arrested. Washington believed that W.E.B. was behind the incident, even though he wasn't. Washington began openly attacking W.E.B.

Some of the attacks threatened W.E.B.'s livelihood. He said,

> **Atlanta University would not be able to get support for its general work or for its study of the Negro problem so long as I remained at the institution.**

W.E.B. called a meeting of other black leaders. He spelled out its purpose:

> **To oppose firmly present methods of strangling honest criticism; to organize intelligent and honest Negroes; and to support organs of news and public opinion.**

Booker T. Washington was an important author who had been born a slave but became the first black man to work as a school principal. He disagreed with W.E.B. about the need for equal rights and instead stressed the importance of education and job skills for blacks.

THE NIAGARA MOVEMENT

The group met near Niagara Falls in the summer of 1905. The organization that emerged early the following year was the Niagara Movement. Saying that the rights of blacks were steadily decreasing while hatred and discrimination were increasing, W.E.B. stated,

W.E.B. (front, 5th from right) joins other members of the Niagara Movement at a conference in 1906. The group insisted on political, social, and civil rights for blacks. Out of that organization arose the National Association for the Advancement of Colored People, which is still going strong after more than 100 years.

"Against this the Niagara Movement eternally protests. We will not be satisfied to take one jot or tittle less than our full manhood rights. We claim for ourselves every single right that belongs to a freeborn American, political, civil, and social; and until we get these rights we will never cease to protest and **assail** the ears of America."

As if to underscore his points, rioting broke out in Atlanta in the summer of 1906. White mobs attacked blacks throughout the city. Fearing for their safety, W.E.B. sent Nina and Yolande to Great Barrington.

MORE RIOTING

Two years later, a riot erupted in Springfield, Illinois. People of both races were killed and injured. Two things made this disturbance different. One was the fact that it was in a northern city. The other was that Springfield was Abraham Lincoln's burial site.

A group of liberal whites outraged by the riot invited W.E.B. to join them for a conference in New York City in May 1909. He said,

> "This conference contained four groups: scientists who knew the race problem; **philanthropists** willing to help worthy causes; social workers ready to take up a new task of abolition; and Negroes ready to join a new crusade for their **emancipation**."

Notably missing were supporters of Washington. He had continued his attacks on W.E.B., and applied pressure against the Niagara Movement to make sure it would fail. It did, but its spirit carried on in the organization that emerged from the New York conference.

At first this new organization called itself the National Negro Committee. It soon became the National Association for the Advancement of Colored People (NAACP). It would revolutionize the struggle for the rights of blacks.

Chapter
4

A
LONG HISTORY
OF LEADERSHIP

IN 1910, NAACP LEADERS INVITED W.E.B.
to leave Atlanta University and move to their head-
quarters in New York City as director of publicity and
research. It was a momentous decision. No longer
would he be a teacher. Now he would be in the front
lines of the struggle for equality.

W.E.B.'s primary responsibility was editing and publishing
The Crisis, the NAACP's monthly magazine. He made it clear
from the start that the magazine would reflect his own views.
This attitude sometimes brought him into conflict with some
NAACP leaders.

The success of *The Crisis* was phenomenal. Within a few years
its readership approached 100,000.

A similar thing happened with the NAACP. The organization
established branch offices in major cities and attracted thousands
of members.

W.E.B. works in his office at the NAACP as the director of publicity and research. After moving from Atlanta to New York, he began his long tenure as a leader in the fight for racial equality. He used his position at the NAACP to constantly speak out about equal justice for blacks.

For years W.E.B. had been a Republican, the party of Lincoln. In 1911 he joined the **Socialist** Party. He liked their emphasis on the equality of all people.

NAACP: Past and Present

When it was founded, the NAACP combined support from white philanthropists with W.E.B.'s call for racial justice. It became the first successful organization devoted to civil rights.

The primary emphasis of the NAACP has been to work within the U.S. legal system to create social changes. Examples of these changes include full voting rights for blacks and ending racial violence. Its first major victory came in 1954. The Supreme Court's decision in *Brown* v. *Board of Education* outlawed segregation in American schools.

As the civil rights movement gained steam throughout the 1960s, many blacks thought the NAACP was far too conservative. New groups formed, such as the Southern Christian Leadership Conference, headed by Dr. Martin Luther King Jr., which believed in direct action.

The NAACP remains a powerful force today, with more than half a million members. It continues its emphasis on legal action, and in recent years has also worked to improve economic conditions for blacks and education for black youth.

CHANGE OF HEART

A year later, he resigned from the party, though he still believed in its basic principles. He felt the Democratic presidential nominee, Woodrow Wilson, would best help to advance the cause of blacks. Wilson, however, proved to be a severe disappointment after he was elected.

Booker T. Washington died in 1915. W.E.B. replaced him as the leading black voice in the country.

When World War I ended late in 1918, W.E.B. went to Europe to look into the conditions under which black soldiers had served. He stayed there to organize a Pan-African Congress, modeling it after the one he had attended in 1900. The main purpose was to liberate black Africans from colonial rule. He also wanted to emphasize that Africa had a rich cultural heritage. As he wrote several years later,

"Africa appears as the Father of mankind. . . . The sense of beauty is the last and best gift of Africa to the world and the true essence of the Black man's soul."

ANOTHER DISPUTE

Soon afterward W.E.B. became involved in his second major disagreement with a black leader. This one was Marcus Garvey, who formed the Universal Negro Improvement Association (UNIA) in 1914.

Garvey emphasized black pride and advocated a back-to-Africa movement. He said blacks would never be accepted as equals in the United States. Their best hope was returning to their ancestral home.

Garvey made a serious mistake. He joined forces with the Ku Klux Klan. He said that at least blacks knew where they stood with the Klan. Many supporters disagreed. They abandoned him

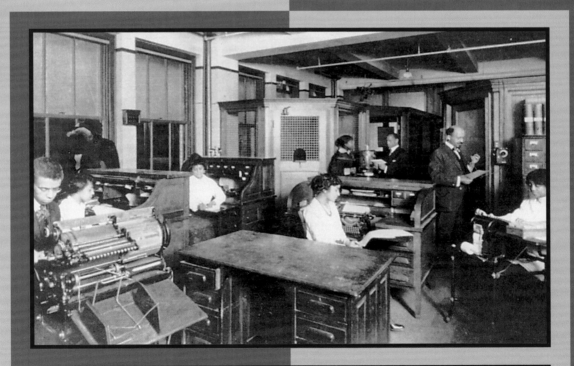

W.E.B. joins other staff in the pressroom of the NAACP magazine, *The Crisis,* in the 1910s. Both the magazine and the NAACP became very successful, and *The Crisis* soon reached 100,000 readers. W.E.B. edited the magazine for almost 25 years.

W.E.B. receives the 1920 NAACP Spingarn Medal, an award for outstanding achievement by a black American. During this time, W.E.B. helped organize a Pan-African Congress in Europe, helped promote the Harlem Renaissance, and visited Russia to study its system of government.

and joined the NAACP. Garvey was convicted of mail fraud in 1925 and deported.

Not everything that W.E.B. did involved political struggle. He also helped to promote the Harlem Renaissance, an outpouring of black music, poetry, and other arts in the 1920s.

He also continued to travel, making several trips overseas. One was to the Soviet Union in 1926. The country had been under communist rule for nearly a decade. W.E.B. was impressed with what he saw:

The Rise of Harlem as a Black Neighborhood

Dutch settlers founded Harlem on Manhattan Island in 1658. For many years Harlem was a small agricultural village. It became part of New York City in 1873.

Many apartments and other buildings were soon constructed. But in the early 1900s, housing prices fell sharply.

By that time, *Plessy* v. *Ferguson* and the increase in Jim Crow laws made it hard for blacks to live in the South. Many moved north, and some came to New York. Harlem's cheap housing encouraged them to settle there. Soon Harlem became the city's most populous black neighborhood.

After World War II, blacks settled in other areas of the city. Harlem was no longer New York's largest black community, but it still is considered the city's leading black cultural and political area.

> **"Russia [the main country in the Soviet Union] was and still is to my mind the most hopeful land in the modern world. . . . Their whole life was being renewed and filled with vigor and ideal."**

A CALL FOR HELP

The Great Depression, which began in 1929, affected W.E.B. *The Crisis* had always been financially independent of the NAACP, allowing him a free editorial voice. Now people couldn't afford it. He went to the NAACP for help.

In return, the NAACP wanted more editorial control. In 1934 W.E.B. wrote an editorial criticizing the policies of executive secretary Walter White. A few weeks later, the NAACP board said no one drawing a salary could criticize officers of the organization. W.E.B. resigned. It wasn't easy. "To give up *The Crisis* was like giving up a child," he wrote.

For a long time, John Hope, president of Atlanta University, had urged W.E.B. to come back. W.E.B. took him up on the offer, especially since Hope told him that his appointment would be for life. At age 66, W.E.B. moved back to Atlanta. His wife refused to go with him. Instand she moved to Baltimore to live with their daughter Yolande.

BIG PLANS

Soon after his arrival W.E.B. began work on one of his pet projects, *The Encyclopedia of the Negro*. It was something he had wanted to do as far back as 1909, but the time demands of his NAACP work and other activities had kept him from working on it.

Noted scholars in the United States, Europe, and Africa promised to write articles. He would devote considerable time (with almost no pay) to the *Encyclopedia* for more than a decade. Ultimately it failed. As he explained,

> **"The necessary funds could not be secured. Perhaps again it was too soon to expect large aid for so ambitious a project directed by Negroes and built mainly on Negro scholarship."**

The *Encyclopedia* wasn't the only writing he did. In 1935 he published one of his most famous books, *Black Reconstruction in America: 1860–1880*. Reconstruction referred to the plan to rebuild the South after the destruction caused by the Civil War.

Up to that point, the prevailing opinion was that Reconstruction failed because blacks weren't ready for the leadership positions they took. Nonsense, W.E.B. said. He blamed its failure on racism and violence. Today his views on Reconstruction are generally accepted.

THE OUTBREAK OF WAR

World War II broke out in September 1939, and the United States became involved in 1941. W.E.B. felt that victory would advance the cause of democracy and create more opportunities for blacks. As had been the case in World War I, tens of thousands of blacks eventually served in the military.

As war raged overseas, W.E.B. wanted to revive his Atlanta conferences. But his plans—and his life—were thrown into disarray when he was asked to retire in 1943. His outspoken views had made many enemies. Hope, the school's president, had died in 1936 and couldn't help him. It was a bitter blow:

W.E.B. (front, 2nd from right) poses with the editorial and advisory boards of *The Encyclopedia of the Negro* in New York City, 1936. He envisioned a huge book containing information on the history, cultures, and social organizations of people of African descent. However, the project was never completed due to lack of funding.

> ❝Without a word of warning I found myself at the age of 76 without employment and with less than $5,000 of savings. . . . [My] life was thrown into confusion. I felt the world tottering beneath my feet and I fought back in despair.❞

RETURN TO THE NAACP

Help came from an unlikely source: the NAACP. The organization wanted someone to help draw the world's attention to the situation of blacks when the war was over.

W.E.B. welcomes a photographer to his home in 1948. During the 1940s he studied how black soldiers had been treated in World War II and helped organize the United Nations. But because he still respected the culture of the communist Soviet Union, he was forced to resign from the NAACP.

Blacks and the Military in World War II

In most cases, blacks serving in World War II were segregated into units led by whites. Often they were assigned tasks that were either dangerous or demeaning.

Despite these limitations, some black units became famous. One was the Tuskegee Airmen. They were black pilots who flew fighter planes in Europe.

Another was the Red Ball Express, a fleet of thousands of trucks that delivered badly needed supplies to advancing American troops in Europe. The personnel were about 75% black.

Military segregation ended in 1948 when President Harry Truman signed Executive Order 9981, though it was six years before the last all-black unit was abolished. Today many people believe the armed forces are one of the most fully integrated elements of American life.

The NAACP sent him to help develop the United Nations in 1945. He also attended the fifth Pan-African Congress, where he was hailed as the organization's father.

He returned to further conflict with the organization, which still expected him to "toe the line" with respect to their official positions. As had been the case before, that was a condition he couldn't accept.

FEAR OF COMMUNISM

There were other problems. W.E.B. still liked the Soviet Union, but millions of Americans feared it. They were especially afraid of "**communist** front" organizations. These were groups secretly controlled by the Communist Party. NAACP leaders felt that if they were closely associated with W.E.B., they might be considered as a communist front.

In 1948, W.E.B. left the NAACP for good. He continued to write in favor of world peace. Many people were suspicious of him. These suspicions deepened when he went to a peace conference in the Soviet Union in 1949.

When he returned, he helped form the Peace Information Center (PIC). It would soon land him in serious trouble.

Chapter
5

❧

LEAVING THE UNITED STATES BEHIND

W.E.B. RECEIVED A SHOCK IN THE SUMMER of 1950. His wife Nina died. Even though they had lived apart for many years, her death was still a blow. Most of his other friends had also died. But he did have the benefit of strong support from a much younger friend, Shirley Graham.

Shirley first met W.E.B. in 1920, when she was just 13 years old. Since then she had been married, had had two sons, and now was a widow. She and W.E.B. had written letters to each other for many years.

W.E.B. needed help. The PIC circulated petitions calling for a halt to building atomic bombs. That made the U.S. government angry. They began investigating W.E.B.

At the same time W.E.B. was approached by the American Labor Party, which asked him to run for the U.S. Senate. As he explained,

W.E.B. and his second wife, Shirley Graham, celebrate their wedding day in 1951. He and Shirley traveled throughout the world advocating peace and socialism, but W.E.B. offended some Americans by his support of communist countries. Eventually he and Shirley decided to leave the United States behind and live overseas.

"I went into the campaign for Senator knowing well from the first that I did not have a ghost of a chance for election, and that my efforts would bring me ridicule at best and jail at worst. On the other hand, I did have a message which was worth attention, and which in the long run could not fail to have influence."

Communist "Witch Hunts" in the United States

The United States and the Soviet Union were allies during World War II. But deep political divisions between the two countries were obvious. As soon as the war ended, the Cold War began. The two countries were hostile but didn't actually fight each other.

Many Americans were very afraid of the Soviet Union. They thought the United States was infested with communist spies and others who wanted to overthrow the U.S. government. Starting in the late 1940s, several Congressional committees began what were called "**witch hunts**." These committees often accused people of having communist connections even without having much evidence against them.

Many of those who were investigated had their reputations and careers destroyed even though they were completely innocent. The witch hunts finally died out in the late 1950s.

A Loss and a Win

To his surprise and delight, he received four percent of the total vote, but that was far short of what he needed. There was another benefit. Shirley Graham worked closely with him, and they were married on Valentine's Day, 1951.

Soon the government put him on trial for his ties with the PIC. He could be fined as much as $10,000 (nearly $90,000 today) and imprisoned for up to five years. He was even briefly handcuffed. The first day in court was especially frightening:

> **"Nothing has so cowed me as that day, November 8, 1951, when I took my seat in a Washington courtroom as an indicted criminal. I was not a criminal. I had broken no law, consciously or unconsciously. Yet I sat with four other American citizens of unblemished character, never before accused even of misdemeanor, in the seats often occupied by murderers, forgers, and thieves."**

Even though Judge James McGuire was politically conservative, he knew a bogus case when he heard one. The government had almost no evidence against W.E.B. McGuire dismissed the charges.

HARD TIMES

W.E.B. was still guilty in the court of public opinion. Fewer people and groups invited him to speak or write. The government took away his passport so he couldn't travel. Perhaps the hardest blow came from the organization he helped found:

> **"The central office of the NAACP refused to let local branches invite me or sponsor any lectures. . . . Even those who disagreed with this judgment at least kept quiet. The colored children ceased to hear my name."**

He refused to give in. Deprived of his leadership among blacks, he shifted his focus. He became even more involved with world

W.E.B. (center) and Shirley (center right) are joined by friends before his trial in 1951. He had been active with the Peace Information Center, and the U.S. government, fearing possible communist ties, put W.E.B. on trial. The charges were later dropped, but his reputation was never the same.

events. He devoted his time to advocating peace, the growth of socialism, and Pan-Africanism.

As always, he continued to write. In 1957, he published *The Ordeal of Mansart.* It was the first book of the Black Flame trilogy. It spans the 80-year life of Manuel Mansart as he has many of the same experiences as the author himself.

GOOD NEWS

As his 90th birthday celebrations showed, many people still honored and revered him. In effect, the Supreme Court gave him a birthday present. The justices made the government return his passport. Now W.E.B. and Shirley could travel.

W.E.B. and Shirley visit Moscow during a worldwide tour in 1959. There W.E.B. received the Lenin Peace Prize. During their year-long travels, he was also honored in China and Uzbekistan. Until the end of his life, W.E.B. continued to focus on world peace and Pan-Africanism.

They spent nearly a year in foreign countries, where they were received far more enthusiastically than in their own country.

In the Soviet Union, Soviet leader Nikita Khrushchev awarded W.E.B. the Lenin Peace Prize. Chinese leader Mao Zedong declared a national holiday in honor of his 91st birthday. In Uzbekistan, W.E.B. attended the Afro-Asian Writers Conference.

AN UNEXPECTED HONOR

Their travels also included the newly independent African nation of Ghana, at the invitation of President Kwame Nkrumah. Nkrumah honored W.E.B. by asking him if he would be interested in producing an *Encyclopaedia Africana*.

Ghana

Ghana is named for an ancient empire of the same name. This empire flourished in Western Africa from about 400 to 1250. It was located a few hundred miles northwest of modern-day Ghana.

Starting in the late 1400s, European traders began arriving in what is now Ghana and neighboring regions. They built forts and searched for gold, giving the name of Gold Coast to the area. Europeans also began the trade in slaves, most of whom they transported to the American continent.

The Ashanti Empire arose in the Gold Coast about 1700. The original Ashantis had left the Empire of Ghana and moved southward.

The British conquered the Gold Coast in the late 1800s, and it became a British colony in 1896. Under the leadership of Kwame Nkrumah, in 1957 Ghana was the first European colony south of the Sahara Desert to become an independent country.

Today Ghana is one of Africa's most stable countries. It is a democracy with a population of more than 23 million.

This was virtually the same project as the *Encyclopedia of the Negro*, which he had been forced to give up years earlier. This time there would be no problem with funds. On the other hand, W.E.B. was 92. Old age was catching up with him. And he would have to leave the United States.

While it was devastating, one of his few remaining U.S. ties was broken when his daughter Yolande suffered a heart attack in 1961 and died.

LEAVING THE UNITED STATES

W.E.B. moved to Ghana later that same year. As a final act of defiance, W.E.B. joined the Communist Party. Even though he had long held communist beliefs, he had never officially been a party member.

He became a citizen of Ghana in February 1963. The University of Ghana gave him an honorary doctorate a few days later, when he turned 95. But his health was declining. He finally had to set aside his work on the *Encyclopaedia Africana*.

He died peacefully on August 27, 1963, at the age of 95. There was a huge state funeral in his honor. President Nkrumah went on nationwide radio to praise him. Tributes poured in from all over the world. There was one notable exception: the government of the United States.

Johnson to Johnson

In an historical oddity, W.E.B. was born during the term of one President Johnson and died a few months before the start of the term of another President Johnson.

Andrew Johnson became president in April, 1865, when Abraham Lincoln was assassinated. Lyndon Johnson became president just over 98 years later when John F. Kennedy was assassinated.

Most people believe that Lincoln did more for blacks than any other president.

Unfortunately, Andrew Johnson did little to continue Lincoln's work.

Many people feel that Lyndon Johnson was nearly as important as Lincoln in promoting civil rights. Though he was from the South, he was responsible for the Civil Rights Act of 1964 and the Voting Rights Act of 1965. These are two of the most important pieces of equal rights legislation in this country's history. He also appointed the first black Supreme Court Justice, Thurgood Marshall.

A LASTING LEGACY

Ironically, the famous March on Washington—at that time the largest civil rights gathering ever—began the day after W.E.B.'s death. The crowd observed a moment of silence in his honor. For famed magazine editor Ralph McGill, the timing was more than coincidental:

W.E.B. meets the Ghanian ambassador in New York in 1961. After the president of Ghana invited him to create an encyclopedia of Africa, W.E.B. left the U.S. and moved to Ghana. He became a Ghanian citizen in 1963 and died there six months later.

"One could not help experiencing a feeling of destiny linking both events. The man who for many years had spoken with the loudest and most articulate voice was now silent while his objectives were being realized."

Reverend Howard Melish, a longtime friend of W.E.B., was part of the huge crowd. He said,

Dr. Martin Luther King Jr. salutes the crowd during the March on Washington, 1963. King's dedication to civil rights was inspired by W.E.B.'s focus on the cause of social justice. W.E.B.'s influence has continued down the generations, and his legacy is clear as America celebrates the election of its first biracial president.

> **"A woman was overheard to cry out, 'It's just like Moses. He was never given to enter the Promised Land.' For myself, I wondered. Perhaps he was, in the sense he coveted. For every informed person in that greatest throng ever gathered in a demonstration in our nation's capital knew that it was the end result of his inspiration."**

History professor Allen B. Ballard said,

> **"Without a doubt, I would consider him [W.E.B.] the most important African American of the whole last century. He dominates everything."**

PRAISE FROM MARTIN LUTHER KING JR.

Dr. Martin Luther King Jr. paid tribute to W.E.B. in 1968 on the 100th anniversary of his birth in what—tragically—was the last major address of King's life:

> **"History cannot ignore W.E.B. Du Bois because history has to reflect truth and Dr. Du Bois was a tireless explorer and a gifted discoverer of social truths. His singular greatness lay in his quest for truth about his own people. . . . The degree to which he succeeded disclosed the great dimensions of the man."**

W.E.B. Du Bois dedicated his life to social justice and always stood up for what he believed in. With the nation having just elected its first biracial president, his views are more relevant than ever.

1868   William Edward Burghardt (usually abbreviated W.E.B.) Du Bois born to Mary Burghardt and Alfred Du Bois on February 23 in Great Barrington, Massachusetts.

1884   Graduates from high school.

1885   Enters Fisk University.

1888   Graduates from Fisk University; enters Harvard University.

1890   Receives B.A. degree from Harvard.

1892   Begins two years of European travel and study at the University of Berlin.

1894   Becomes professor of classics at Wilberforce University in Ohio.

1895   Receives Ph.D. from Harvard.

1896   Marries Nina Gomer; takes one-year position at the University of Pennsylvania.

1897   Becomes professor of history and economics at Atlanta University; son Burghardt Gomer Du Bois is born.

1899   Son dies of diphtheria; *The Philadelphia Negro* is published.

1900   Appointed secretary of first Pan-African Congress, held in London, England; daughter Yolande is born.

1903   Publishes *The Souls of Black Folk: Essays and Sketches*.

1905   Organizes Niagara Movement to challenge Booker T. Washington's leadership of blacks.

1909   Serves as one of the founders of the National Association for the Advancement of Colored People (NAACP).

1910   Appointed NAACP director of publicity and research; begins publishing NAACP monthly magazine, *The Crisis*.

1911   Joins Socialist Party but leaves it a year later.

1919   Helps organize Pan-African Congress.

1926   Visits the Soviet Union.

1934	Resigns from NAACP and returns to Atlanta University.
1935	Publishes *Black Reconstruction in America: 1860–1880.*
1939	Publishes *Black Folk Then and Now: An Essay in the History and Sociology of the Negro Race.*
1944	Forced to retire from Atlanta University; returns to NAACP.
1945	Becomes part of U.S. delegation at the founding of the United Nations.
1950	Wife Nina dies; becomes candidate of American Labor Party for U.S. Senate from New York.
1951	Marries Shirley Graham; put on trial but is quickly acquitted.
1952	Publishes *In Battle For Peace: The Story of My 83rd Birthday, With Comment by Shirley Graham.*
1957	Publishes *The Ordeal of Mansart.*
1958	Celebrates 90th birthday at Roosevelt Hotel in New York City and other locations.
1959	Travels around the world and meets with leaders Nikita Khrushchev, Mao Zedong, as well as Ghana's president Kwame Nkrumah.
1961	Daughter dies; emigrates to Ghana.
1963	Becomes citizen of Ghana; dies on August 27.

1884	W.E.B. Du Bois delivers speech at high school graduation.
1890	Delivers speech at Harvard commencement.
1895	Becomes the first black to receive a Ph.D. degree from Harvard University.
1900	Wins gold medal for his Negro Exhibit at the Paris Exposition, a world's fair.
1909	Becomes the first black to address the annual meeting of the American Historical Association.
1910	Founds *The Crisis*, the official publication of the NAACP, and edits it for 24 years.
1920	Receives NAACP's Spingarn Medal, awarded annually for outstanding achievement by a black American.
1924	Honored for his efforts in Pan-Africanism by more than 500 prominent people at a dinner in New York City.
1930	Receives honorary doctorate degree from Howard University.
1938	Receives honorary doctorate degree from Atlanta University.
	Receives honorary doctorate degree from Fisk University.
1939	Becomes incorporating member of the Society of American Historians.
	Is invited to speak at annual meeting of the Southern Sociological Society.
1940	Receives honorary doctorate degree from Wilberforce University.
1942	Speaks to student bodies of Yale University and Vassar College.
1948	Delivers memorial address to national convention of Sigma Pi Phi, association of notable professional black men.
1958	Becomes member of Fisk University chapter of Phi Beta Kappa.
1958	Receives honorary doctorate degrees from Charles University in Czechoslovakia, Humboldt University in Berlin, and Moscow State University in the Soviet Union.

1959   China declares his 91st birthday as a national holiday.

Receives Lenin Peace Prize from the Soviet Union.

1963   Receives first honorary doctorate degree awarded by the University of Ghana.

1992   United States Postal Service issues a stamp in his honor.

1994   Main library at the University of Massachusetts at Amherst is named for him.

2006   Du Bois Center for American History opens in Great Barrington.

alleged—something claimed to be true but without definite proof.

assail—attack.

chancellor—chief minister of state in some countries in Europe.

commencement—graduation ceremony at a school.

communist—person who believes in a form of government in which a single party controls the economy and distributes goods equally.

culminated—reached an ending or decisive point.

diphtheria—disease that attacks the heart and nervous system.

doctoral dissertation—long research paper that is a requirement to get a Ph.D. degree.

emancipation—freedom from bondage.

indicted—charged with a crime.

Jim Crow laws—laws that discriminate against blacks; supposedly named after a song and dance routine that featured white actors in blackface.

menial—humble, lowly.

philanthropists—people who donate money to causes or organizations whose aims and objectives they support.

premier—the prime minister of a country.

ramshackle—rickety; on the verge of collapsing.

sharecroppers—people who work land belonging to someone else and give that person a portion of the crops they grow.

socialist—belief that there is no private property; the government owns the means of production and all people are equal.

vanguard—someone or something that is at the front of a movement.

witch hunts—attacking people with unpopular beliefs.

Books

Bolden, Tonya. *W.E.B. Du Bois* (Up Close). New York: Viking Juvenile, 2008.

Gillis, Jennifer Blizin. *W.E.B. Du Bois* (American Lives). Chicago: Heinemann, 2005.

Hinman, Bonnie. *A Stranger In My Own House: The Story Of W. E. B. Du Bois* (Portraits of Black Americans). Greensboro, North Carolina: Morgan Reynolds, 2005.

Randolph, Ryan P. *W.E.B. Du Bois: The Fight for Civil Rights* (The Library of American Lives & Times). New York: Rosen Publishing Group, 2005.

Stafford, Mark and John Davenport. *W.E.B. Du Bois: Scholar and Activist* (Black Americans of Achievement). Philadelphia: Chelsea House, 2005.

Troy, Don. *W.E.B. Du Bois* (Journey to Freedom). Mankato, Minnesota: Child's World, 2009.

Web Sites

http://www.library.umass.edu/spcoll/dubois/

This collection of materials relating to W.E.B. Du Bois includes brief biography, timeline, and many photographs.

http://www.naacp.org/

The Web site of the National Association for the Advancement of Colored People includes history, a timeline, and links related to W.E.B. Du Bois.

http://www.lucidcafe.com/library/96feb/dubois.html

This site includes a very brief biography, photos, a list of books by and about W.E.B. Du Bois, additional Web sites, and more.

http://www.webdubois.org/

This collection includes many links about W.E.B. Du Bois and his own writing.

PICTURE CREDITS

ABOUT THE AUTHOR

Jim Whiting has written more than 100 children's non-fiction books and edited well over 150 more during an especially diverse writing career. He published *Northwest Runner* magazine for more than 17 years. His other credits include advisor to a national award–winning high school newspaper, sports editor for the *Bainbridge Island Review*, event and venue write-ups and photography for American Online, articles in dozens of magazines, light verse in the *Saturday Evening Post*, the first piece of original fiction to appear in *Runner's World*, and official photographer for the Antarctica Marathon. His other Mason Crest titles include *American Idol Judges*, *Troy Polamalu*, *David Beckham*, *Hilary Duff*, and *Mandy Moore*.